A View from the Ground Up

ANGELS
for all
SEASONS

MARTHA RICKEY

Inspiring Voices books may be ordered through booksellers or by contacting:

Inspiring Voices
1663 Liberty Drive
Bloomington, IN 47403
www.inspiringvoices.com
1-(866) 697-5313

Because of the dynamic nature of the Internet, any web addresses or links contained in this book may have changed since publication and may no longer be valid. The views expressed in this work are solely those of the author and do not necessarily reflect the views of the publisher, and the publisher hereby disclaims any responsibility for them.

Any people depicted in stock imagery provided by Thinkstock are models, and such images are being used for illustrative purposes only.

Certain stock imagery © Thinkstock.

ISBN: 978-1-4624-0075-1 (sc)

Library of Congress Control Number: 2012933905

Printed in the United States of America

Inspiring Voices rev. date: 04/23/2012

Dedication

To all the angels, visible and otherwise, who guided my hands and feet and sent me on this incredible journey.

Angels of God

Angel of God, my guardian dear,
To whom God's love commits me here;
Ever this day be at my side,
To light and love, to rule and guide.

A simple prayer learned in elementary school,
Which when recited daily becomes a living tool.
But the years pass by and the travails of life,
Makes one forget that lesson, due to toil and strife.

But then one day at the cemetery gate,
I encountered what is known as an act of fate.
No matter where I looked to my left or my right,
I beheld a calming…and beautiful sight.

There to be seen, by each visiting guest,
Are examples of how God's faithful are blessed.
He has arranged as a sign through his grace and concern,
For His Angels to be seen at every turn.

To one who believes, while each IS made of stone,
They bring a message of peace, that we're never alone.
God's carriers of love are at their best,
Standing by our loved one's in their final rest.

And assuring us as we visit to pray,
That those we remember will always stay
Protected by God through these sentinels of love,
As if standing guard though their souls be above.

Jack Carroll

Contents

Foreward

by Cynthia Dukes, Intuitive Healer, Reiki Master and Psychic

I believe without knowing it, Martha Rickey started creating this book a long time ago. I believe the angels specifically picked Martha to be the one to create it. It appears that they lead her every step of the way.

When Martha and I spent time together, sooner or later the subject would turn to angels. There were always little reminders that the angels were around. Sitting in a restaurant a small white feather would float down onto our table out of nowhere. On one particularly stressful day at work a feather appeared on a table in a room where Martha was working, even though the windows were locked. Strangers would strike up conversations with us about angels. Shopkeepers would tell us angel stories. It seemed as though the topic of angels was always around. One day a woman who owned an angel shop began to show us pictures of clouds that she had taken and they were all in the shape of angels. Martha thought this was great and shared her stories about taking pictures of statues of angels.

Martha had, what I thought at first was strange, a habit of visiting cemeteries and taking pictures of angels. She had pictures of angels from all seasons. One winter when we had a very bad snowfall, I decided to give Martha a call and see how bad the weather was in her neighborhood. To my surprise, while most people were safe in their warm houses, Martha was in the cemetery taking more angel pictures. Her feet and her intuition took her there, no questions asked.

Then the angel experiences began to grow. We would go on road trips and while walking in some little town there would be statues of angels in parks, outside churches, public buildings and even in people's yards. They were everywhere and Martha was there with her camera. It was as if the angels were saying, "Hey, we're here! We're all around you! Take our pictures!" They were truly calling her.

One particular day I took a trip with Martha to a local cemetery. I watched in the stillness of that cemetery how she came alive with her camera. She knew what statue to choose, what angle to use, how to shoot a picture from below or from the side, how the sun hit the stone, or the beauty of seeing an angel through the branches of a tree. It was beautiful. It was almost as if they were showing her where to go and what to do. How she captured the beauty of each statue in every season was amazing. She made them all come alive.

When she finally decided to create this little book, it was difficult to decide which pictures she would choose. As I helped her go through the pictures, something happened. As I stared at each picture, I experienced such a feeling of peace and love. The beauty of each picture brought to me an awareness that these angels truly do exist. Each time I would look at the photos I would find myself feeling lighter and lighter and realized that I had a smile on my face from ear to ear.

I urge you to use this little book to connect with the angels. I believe they truly want that. As you reach out to the angels, I am sure you will begin to have your very own experience of angels in your life.

From the bottom of my heart, I would like to thank Martha for creating this book and the delightful and funny experiences we shared along this journey. I am sure the angels will continue to cheer her on.

Preface

Angels for all Seasons started with a neighborhood walk one snowy day. After wandering through the local park I found myself outside the gates of one of the cemeteries in my neighborhood. It is a very old cemetery with a lot of statuary. Having walked quite a distance through the snowstorm, I was already cold and tired. However, my feet seemed to be acting independently of my brain and had other plans for me. They guided me to a section of the cemetery where there were many beautiful angels who were covered in snow.

Standing in the snow, in utter silence, I was struck by the abject loneliness of the angels around me. They were all cloaked in soft, snowy blankets of white. With the wind whipping the falling snow around me, I removed my camera from the plastic bag and started taking photos of the snowy sentinels. Only after uploading the photos to my computer, did I realize how much the snow added to their beauty.

I continued to document the beauty of my snow angels throughout the winter months. With the welcomed arrival of spring, I felt compelled to return to the cemeteries to check up on the guardians of our loved ones. My timing was a little premature because the trees were just starting to form their little buds. At the same time an idea was forming in my mind; photograph the angels each season to highlight their beauty throughout the year! As one season changed into the next, I was out photographing my favorite subjects, the angels. Thus began the inspiration for *Angels for all Seasons*.

Since amassing a huge collection of angel photos, I have spent countless hours studying their beauty, their demeanor, their hands and their wings. Visiting these angels throughout the year gave me a peaceful feeling. I connected to them on many different levels. Every season provided me with a different prospective. I felt as if the angels themselves were speaking directly to me each time I paid them a visit.

Choosing who goes into *Angels for all Seasons* was a difficult task since all angels are beautiful. I have managed to choose some of my favorites. I hope you will enjoy them as much as I do.

Introduction

Angels for all Seasons was created as a starting point for meditation, contemplation or just relaxation. The photos within, combined with your own meditations, will hopefully help you to connect with your spiritual self.

Chapter 1

SPRING

Flowers come up to
herald the onset of the
spring of our lives.

Chapter 2

SUMMER

Summer flowers watch
your bed of eternal rest
and guide you through sleep.

Chapter 3

FALL

As you are asleep
another season arrives
that you will not see.

Chapter 4

WINTER

During the cold night
winter snow blankets the ground
where you are at rest.

Afterward

It is hoped that when you finish *Angels for all Seasons* you will be inspired to see the beauty of the cemetery sentinels in a different light.

CPSIA information can be obtained
at www.ICGtesting.com
Printed in the USA
LVIW012105010512

279935LV00001B